FROM THE HEART
......Lesson From A Sparrow

Written by Sandra Jackson

1stBooks - rev. 04/30/01

Dedication

In loving memory of my beautiful mother, Mildred Lawson. Her love and encouragement has guided and lifted my life. Even to this day, her love inspires me to reach for my dreams. Miss you Mom.

In loving memory of my wonderful father and mother in-law, Joe and Mildred Jackson. Their love and support has been very much appreciated in my life. Miss you Mom and Pop Jackson.

To Michael, my wonderful husband of 18 years. Also to my three great sons, Mike, Joshua and Jonathan, who are all my heart and the wind beneath my wings.

To my loving father, Elder Nathaniel Lawson; who always tells me, my writing is a gift from God.

Last but certainly not least, to Bill, Garfield, Bob and Horace Lawson. My four loving and giving brothers who are (and have always been) a vital part of my life.

I love you all and to God be the glory!

Sandra Jackson

Lesson From A Sparrow

Sandra Jackson

Lesson From A Sparrow

I watched a little sparrow

As I was sitting in my car,

He attempted to cross a busy street

Which to him seemed Oh so far!

One minute he would hop along

But then would have to retreat,

Trying this over and over again

To make his journey complete

As I watched in amazement and disbelief

I wondered why he hopped,

For he so easily could have flown

And brought his worries to a stop

Then God patted me on the shoulder

And said, "I wonder the same about you,

Instead of mounting up with wings as eagles

You hop across things you go through

I love you much more than the sparrow

For you I became the Christ,

Let me bare your burdens and trials

So you can fly your way across life!"

When God Says No

God loves us dearly and sometimes in prayer

His answer is "no" because He really cares,

He can see things that are afar off

We can only see what it is that we want

He loves us enough to sometimes say "no"

For all things we ask, will not help us grow,

His love for us is as a father to a child

That's why I'll take all things in stride

Just think how miserable we would all be

If God merely said, "go do as you please,"

Yes, we would be as forsaken children

Receiving no love or sense of discipline

So whatever state I find myself in

I'll be content and continue to the end,

My prayers and praises will forever flow

Thank God He loves us enough to say "no."

I'm Blessed

Blessed when I stand and

Blessed when I kneel,

Blessed when I'm well and

Blessed when I'm ill

Blessed in the morning when I rise

Blessed at bedtime and should I die,

Blessed in the midst of a raging storm

Blessed when it's bright and clouds are gone

Blessed when tears fill my eyes

Blessed when I'm happy and with a smile,

Blessed when it seems I'm at my end

Blessed when He renews my strength again

Blessed because God's never far away

Blessed because He hears me when I pray,

Blessed because He saved my soul from sin

Blessed because Jesus is my best friend.

"Noth'n For My Journey"

Long ago, old saints would say

"I wouldn't take noth'n for my journey,"

With respect, I would smile and nod

Though I didn't have full understanding

Many years have come and gone

Each lesson learned, "heaven sent,"

I've grown through all my tests and trials

Finally, I know what they meant

I wouldn't give anything for one tear

That ran down on my face,

Because it taught me to lean on God, and

Never give up in haste

I wouldn't give anything for one pain

My body, in sickness would feel,

Each showed me the beauty of God's stripes

Also to know that He's real

So now that I am middle aged

And have learned; and yet learning still,

"I wouldn't take noth'n for my journey"

If you've never said it – you will!

Like A Tree

Like a tree standing, beside a river

I shall stand and shall not wither,

My branches shall, reach out to those

Whose hearts are crying for answers untold

My roots shall be planted, deep in God's word

So when winds blow, I'll stand assured,

Lord let my leaves be shade for all

Who need relief from the stress of this world

At night let me stand quiet and still

Resting and listening for your will,

Like a tree, let me be, strong and mute

Showing forth your praises, by my fruit.

The Dream

I had a dream one night while sleeping

That people in Spanish were yelling and chanting,

They yelled at me, "Castras!" in a loud voice

Just as though I had no choice

I had never heard of the word they spoke

Yet for some reason my faith would not choke,

I then began to counter attack, and

Yelled, I love the Lord and I won't take it back!

My husband awoke me for I made some noise

When I explained it to him he advised ask our boys,

My children told me just what "Castras" meant

"To constrain, hold back or try to prevent"

At first I thought it regarded healing

But it wasn't about how my body was feeling,

There was a message much stronger than that

One that would help me fill in the gap

Now I know for certain and sure

God was telling me to endure, and

No matter how the odds are stacked

I <u>must</u> love the Lord and not take it back!

Your Instrument

Lord I give you the glory, for everything good in my life

Before you saved my soul one day, I had no cure for strife,

Now I can get down on my knees, and cry out to you Lord

For you have given me your love, and it's called the comforter

Every good and perfect gift, cometh from above

Therefore my abilities, come only through your love,

I can not boast or brag, about anything I've done

That would be like saying, a father was born of his son

When you enable me to do, those things that bring you praise

My heart and hands in unison, are automatically raised,

They're raised because I'm giving, all the glory and honor to

you

For I am merely the instrument, that you decided to use.

Miracles

I was in need of a miracle

My need for one was grave,

Satan slyly convinced me though

They existed only in Jesus' days

Then something strange soon happened

My memory began to speak,

"Remember the times you were sick

Yet God strengthened what was weak"

"Or the nights you laid awake

Your trials seemed much too great,

Only to make it through them all

With a mustard seed of faith"

"How 'bout each morning you arise

Deep breaths of air you take,

Ability to move both arms and legs

No sense does satan make!"

With amusement I then shook my head, and

Picked up a mirror to see,

Miracles <u>do</u> exist today

I'm looking at one – it's me!

Automatic Praise

Just as a leg lifts quickly

When a doctor taps its knee,

In times of sun or trouble

Let my praises lift to thee

Let it be automatic

Without hesitation or thought,

Instill praise within my spirit,

With joy, let every battle be fought

Help me appreciate good times

Yet when the tough times come,

Keep me ever grateful

Praying let thy will be done

Let it be a reflex, Lord

This thankfulness in me,

No matter what situation arise

My praise belongs to thee.

Thanksgiving is Here!

Thanksgiving is here once again!

But this year I've made a decision,

To not only thank God for the good

But for the bad and for whatever's missing

I thank God for illnesses that I have faced

For through them I've learned to lean,

Wholly on Christ who's always there

Even though He's never seen

I also thank Him for burdens and trials

For through them God made me strong,

He taught me that I can depend on Him

As I lean on His everlasting arms

I also thank Him for what might be missing

Whether it's health or finance,

See, God holds them both in the palm of His hand

He's just waiting for me to request them

Thanksgiving is here once again!

Yet it feels like my very first one,

I thank the Lord for both good and bad

But mostly for sending His Son!

How Christmas Was Meant To Be

Christmas comes only once a year

But how often does Christ come to us?

Whenever we're sick or burdened

He's been a very present help

For what if Christ showed love towards us

Only on December 25th?

We would be most miserable

On this earth who's riches are His

So instead of waiting for one special day

To show how much we care,

Let us come to one another's aide

And show love each day of the year

You'll find your life will be merrier

And hopefully you will see,

Loving others as Christ, shows love towards us

Is how Christmas was meant to be.

Another Year

Father you have blessed us, to see another year

We overcame obstacles and conquered all our fears,

All along you protected us, and took, us through the storms

Sent us down your latter rain, and kept us from death's harm

You remained faithful, through 365 days

Taught us how to love, and acknowledge you in our ways,

Many said we wouldn't make it, to the other side

Yet here we stand delivered, for in your word we hide

As the years come and go, we'll always look to you

To direct our path everyday, in all we say and do,

No one knows except you, just what the future holds

Except to say the half of it, has never yet been told

Thank you for another year, you blessed us to see

Keep us holding steadfast and claiming victory,

Not everyone, knows the fact, it's not by power or might

But it's only by your Spirit, we're found pleasing in your sight.

L – asting affection through good times and bad

O – vercoming obstacles and more than a fad

V – ictorious loyalty throughout the years

E - ncouraging always and never with fear

This Valentine's Day our hearts we'll extend

But it was Jesus who laid down His life for a friend,

So honor each other but keep this in mind

That Godly love is the very best kind.

He Arose

Yes, Christ arose one early 'morn

From a dark and dreary grave,

He arose without that thorny crown

For He had made death and sin behave

Now His crown is full of glory and grace

He reigns forever more,

Love and seek Him – please make haste

He's knocking at your door

Not only did He arise from the grave

He also arose in me,

He renewed my mind and now I'm saved

Thank God for victory!

Resurrected

After Jesus had suffered on the cross

Satan thought he had put Him to death,

But God was working things out for us

He merely responded to being in flesh

When satan came again to boast and brag

To the place he had laid Him to rest,

He found that Jesus had been resurrected

For He victoriously passed His test

So, this is what happens to you and I

When we go through trials and stress,

Satan says, "Atlas! I have them!

I know I've gained their death"

Yet when he comes back, to where we should be

To see how we've been effected,

God has already worked things out

That's right, we've been resurrected!!

Mistaken Will

Once trouble came into my life like a flood

And I didn't quite handle it all like I should,

Tried it my way Oh, several times

Lord, I mistook my will for thine

Your will told me to drop to my knees

Yet I said a song is all that I need,

When the situation really got absurd

I realized I needed prayer and your word

In your word, you told me to hold fast

To press toward the mark, and not look to the past,

As I prayed and sought you even more

You delivered my soul and evened the score

Then you told me that wasn't enough

I had to defeat satan and take back my stuff,

Now I've learned to submit to your will, and

Keep pressing on up, life's rugged hill.

Am I A Thorn?

Am I a thorn upon your rose

Your Church purchased with blood?

Lord, am I responsible for hindering growth

With slothfulness and unconcern?

Do I neglect my stewardship

When all must push the plow?

Have I relentlessly given my service, or

Withheld it with, "I don't know how"

Am I a thorn upon your rose

Pushing gossip by word of mouth, or

Simply do I store it within

Hiding hate and distrust in my heart

Do I turn deaf ears unto the truth

When the man of God cries loud?

Knowing he preaches not of himself

But whatsoever saith the Lord

Hear my earnest prayer Lord

Make this only my delight,

To be a small rose petal

Nourished by the begotten Son's light.

Father Forgive Me

Father forgive me when I pray

If I have hurt someone today,

Lord, I do the best I can

Not to offend my fellow man

Sometimes Lord, it seems so hard

Cause everyone hasn't, taken this charge,

Yet and still you make it easy

For you are the one, that I am pleasing

Let the words of my mouth, glorify you

As well as everything that I do,

However, those times I miss the mark

Teach me Savior and don't depart

For without you, I can not stand

Or make it through this barren land,

I want to love others, as you love me

Forgiving and living in victory!

Perhaps

Perhaps together we can explore

This world of mysteries, love and war,

Understand what we can – learn what we don't know

Together my children we can grow

Perhaps together we can grasp

Our untold dreams and make them last, and

Although these dreams may not be the same

Together each one will be attained

Perhaps together as time goes on

We'll light the world up with a song,

A song without music, a song without verse

But together my children we'll make it be heard.

To my son, Michael

A Gift From Heaven

To me it's simply amazing

I can't even find the words,

To describe the joy and pride we felt

When at first your cry was heard

Right away we could tell

You'd be special, in the world,

For you were <u>our</u>, very first child

Unlike other boys and girls

Now here you stand before us

Yes, almost a man,

One who's smart and responsible

Just like the Master planned, and

Just as on that very first day

Our hearts still beam with pride,

For God gave us a gift from heaven, and

You were placed inside.

To my sons: Joshua and Jonathan

T – reasured moments daily unfold

W – isdom blossums as we become old

I – f replaced by optimistic whens

N – urtured little boys can become strong men

S – omeday the families you have – will add

The same happiness which you've given me and Dad!!

Sandra Jackson

Happy Birthday Mom

There's a person we care, there's a person we trust

She is our mother and she cares for us,

Our mother is great, truthful, and kind

The Lord has blessed us to stand by her side,

We journeyed so far and accomplished so much

But there's so much to do and lives to touch,

We love the woman and so does dad

The next time he sees her he'll be so so glad,

We can go so far without a mother's love

For when we are sick she's like a dove,

She helped put God in our lives

She told us to be saved and baptized,

We tell this to you for this is a fact

She's been there for us and that is that.

Written and given with love by,

Michael, Joshua and Jonathan Jackson

December 7, 1997

One Touch

While traveling one day, in a car with my son

I said something like, one day when I'm gone…,

He then grabbed my hand and didn't let go

He held it for about an hour or so

I thought to myself, how very nice

For something that I'd done, had touched his life,

Fourteen years old, yet he had grasped

Love for family that won't ever pass

I use to wonder, will my best be enough

Yet he answered that question, with just one touch,

My job as mother will never be done

But he let me know, he wants no other one.

Our Seed

Our union was blessed in '85 and'83

For our children were a blessing from above,

We showed them your way both night and day

And prayed you'd cover them with love

As toddlers and tots they grew and learned

Just playing as normal kids do,

Sunday school had a big effect on their life

For your word was a heavenly food

Their minds were troubled when they turned teens

For they asked us questions about you,

They wanted to walk as they had been taught

And to know that salvation was true

So one Sunday morning, they went down in your name

You washed away, all of their sins,

You filled each one with your precious Holy Ghost

For they spoke as you entered in

Lord we thank you, for this great miracle

For you said you would bless our seed,

We're a saved family now, just living for you

Oh, great is thy faithfulness indeed!

As for me, this is my convenant with them, saith the

Lord; My spirit that is upon thee, and my words which

I have put in thy mouth, shall not depart out of thy

mouth, nor out of the mouth of thy seed, nor out of the

mouth of thy seed's seed, saith the Lord, from hence-

Forth and for ever. Isaiah 59:21

A Best Friend

When I asked the Lord for a husband

He gave me a best friend,

Someone I could have and hold, and

Depend on till the end

A friend is much more priceless

Than a man who's just your spouse,

For it takes a closer relationship

To have a home, not just a house

That's what your love has given me

Plus, security and peace of mind,

You surround my world with laughter, and

I'll love you till the end of time.

43

Sandra Jackson

To my husband, Michael

Our Love

Growing deeper than I ever thought

Love that passion seems to have caught,

Love without a limited peak

Sustaining us should we become weak

Only to have and hold onto you

Makes each day one to go through,

Growing desires and vanishing fears

Our love, my love, will endure passing years.

Would You?

Would you have done what Moses did?

Give back all those riches of his?

Just to please our mighty God

In exchange, for no more than a rod

Pharaoh had given him a breastplate of gold

Yet the garments God gave him, were ragged and old,

He had thousands at his command

But he became a servant, led by God's own hand

Pharaoh's chariots, use to carry him to and fro

But then by foot, did he walk for the Lord of Host,

Everything in life, that was precious to him

Couldn't out way Egypt's, dark and mighty sin

He knew in his heart, God wanted no slaves

So for this cause, his sacrifices were made,

God delivered Israel to a better land

Would you have been like Moses, and taken a stand?

In Memory Of................

PaPa

Since I can remember Papa has been

A loving grandfather who preached against sin,

He taught me something not easy to find

How to give to others, yet give God your mind

He lovingly gave me his time and advice

Always stern but at the same time nice,

I remember when I first learned to drive

He taught me how to park and arrive alive

He lived through the times when America was dark

Yet God had lit in him, an eternal spark,

This spark was love, patience, and truth

He taught it to his children and grandchildren too

Not very often do you find a man

Who preaches morals and takes a stand,

He's gone on now but I'll never forget

Those precious memories of Bishop Sandy Dunlap.

Sandra Jackson

Mildred and Joe Jackson

Greatly Missed

It's easy to show someone love

When things are going great,

Yet when things get a little rough

That's when true love has faith

My mother and father in law are gone

God called them home to rest,

They always showed me genuine love

Especially during life's tests

With this poem I'd like to say

They are so greatly missed,

Their greatest gift to me was this

Their wonderful son and our kids.

My Uncle Joe

Faithful in word and

Faithful in deed

Lord my uncle meant so much to me

Loving in spirit and

Diligent in prayer

He touched the lives of people everywhere

A minister of music, and a

Singer of songs

Whenever he sang, he made the weak strong

Remembered for his patience and

Promises kept

Once again I understand why Jesus wept.

Auntie

The definition of what's sweet and kind

Auntie was that way all the time,

Someone who always offered a smile

Quiet in spirit yet determined to strive

She fought the good fight of faith

Few words spoken but full of grace,

She knew she had a race to run

Never denying God's only Son

She'll be missed most, for all her kind deeds

Always loving and never mean,

I asked the Lord why her life was short

And He simply said, "She'll rise first."

My Cousin Deborah

When I was at the age of about fourteen

My cousin Deborah helped give me wings,

She taught me how to respect myself, and

Honor God before anything else

I grew up without a natural sister

But she was there, to advise and minister,

She taught me all about, "fast young dudes"

What they would say and sometimes do

Now that I am grown, with kids of my own

I look back in thanks, for the seeds she had sown,

She took the time out, to help and guide me

That's why as a sister, she will always be.

Thanks for the Memories

It's strange what things you remember when you were once a child. Sometimes it's the warmth of the sun. Sometimes it's a taste or a smell. One of the things I remember most, happened one evening when I was about ten years old.

My family and I lived in Up-State New York. It was beautiful there. At that time, which was before VCR's and Nintendo, it was a kid's paradise for adventure. There were trees to climb, woods to be explored and ponds to catch frogs in. We were one of the few Black families who lived on our street. We didn't have much at that time. Our house bore witness of that. It was clean and the yard was always blooming with flowers, thanks to my mom. But compared to the other houses on our street, it just wasn't as modern as the rest.

That late fall evening a young White man had been drinking and driving. He apparently lost control of his car and had crashed into a tree. This all happened about a quarter of a mile from our house. The young man was able somehow to make his way out of his car. He was bleeding profusely and was in desperate need of medical attention. The first house he went to (one of the modern houses mind you) refused to come to the door, considering the lateness of the hour. Obviously in pain, the man proceeded to the next modern house. He was again denied help. That's when he walked for about a quarter of a mile to our humble home; leaving a trail of blood as he stumbled along. When he banged on our door, however, my mom immediately opened it, let him in and began to treat his wounds. Not only did she try to stop the bleeding; she cleaned him up and called for an ambulance.

That next morning all the kids on the bus were praising my mom for what she had done. They also spoke in disbelief of how the other two houses refused to help the young man. My mom was a hero! Though we often struggled to make ends meet; after that night I felt we were one of the richest families around.

Mom was a Christian, but I don't ever recall her passing out tracts or bibles. My mom passed out love. She also taught me that night that it's not what you have that makes you rich. But it's what and how much of yourself you give to others. Thanks mom.

In loving memory of my mother,

Mildred Lawson

Written by, Sandra (Lawson) Jackson

What Now...

From the depths of my soul

Silently pondering through my mind

What now, what now, what now

With all the love he had to give

Yet the color of his skin

Has caused his end, has caused his end, has caused his end

He taught to love and not to fight

Yet a senseless moron took his life

He then took flight out of sight, he then took flight

Should we continue on in peace

Turning still the other cheek

Or should we fight, or should we fight, or should we fight

I'll keep the thoughts of Dr. King

Win this war yet keep it clean

We'll win, yes we'll win

As predicted by Dr. King!

Written by my mother,

The belated Mildred Lawson

On the day Dr. King was killed (1968)

Color

Many gangs take too much pride

In the colors that they wear,

But what they don't realize is

In God's eyes we're all bare

Just look at the children of Israel

Who from the plague was saved,

Because of the blood, upon their posts

Not its color or its shade

Still His blood saves where applied

For that reason and no other,

Under that blood we must abide, and

Stop emphasizing color

Whether we're talking about ones clothes

Or the color of your skin,

We need to have harmony amongst ourselves

So this way we all win.

Softly He Whispers

Softly He whispers His word to me

While I'm standing or on my knees,

He inspires me to always do my best

Not worrying or fretting about the rest

He tells me to hear the praises of those

Who He has loved and preciously chose,

Their testimonies help me to over come

Keeps me hopeful and ready to run

He requires praises from me as well

For in praise He tells me He likes to dwell,

No time for complaining or feeling low

For He's soon to come and with Him I'll go

Softly He whispers His word to me

While I'm standing or on my knees,

Keep me Savior in your care

There are loved ones in glory; I want to meet there.

The Rapture

"How Great Thou Art," has already been sung

Eternity has begun for Jesus has come,

Churches are empty, the choirs are gone

Caught up to meet the Savior, the Eternal One

Chaos has now set in around town

Loved ones are missing and can't be found,

Some sons and daughters are looking for those

Who urged them daily, to get on the right road

Useless promises are made with tears

"Speak to me Jesus," is pleaded with fear,

Yet it's too late for grace has ended

Judgement now waits for satan's descendents

Thank God this all is not the case

There's still time left to run this race,

God loves everyone who hears His voice

Just don't wait till the rapture, to make your choice.

There Will Be Peace In the Valley

(Lyrics)

There will be peace in the valley

There will be joy all around it

There will be peace in the valley

Joy all around it (Repeat Chorus)

(Lead) So many people are living this life

Full of hang ups, burdens and strife

But if they would come to the Master's throne

They would find the peace they need as they travel along

(Repeat Chorus Twice)

(Lead) Sometimes the seas of life get mighty rough

All your friends are gone and you're standing by yourself

But just as He fought the Battle of Jericho

God will fight your enemies and then they will know

(Repeat Chorus Twice)

(Lead) Look at Shadrach, Meshach and Abendego

There were three of them but behold they saw four

In the fiery furnace God cooled the flames and then

They began rejoicing and praising His name

(Repeat Chorus Twice)

Written by, Michael and Sandra Jackson

Romans 8:11

How many times, have you heard

"You can't take it with you,"

Well, let me tell you something about

One thing that disputes that issue

When you were born into this world

God gave His breath of life,

Then when you die, He takes it back

This no man can fight

What if, however, there was something

That though your breath was gone,

Would enable you to one day rise, and

In peace, see God on His throne

Even if death is not your plight, and

The rapture should take place,

What if you had something inside

That would make <u>you</u> a missing case

Thanks be to God there does exist

Just that very thing,

That you can take from earth to glory

Without any tricks or strings

For if the Spirit abides in you

Which also raised Christ from the dead,

It will quicken your mortal body

Just like the scripture said

So don't store up riches on this earth

These things you truly <u>can't</u> take,

Only God's Spirit is travel ready

Obtain it, for your soul's sake!

The Son

Just as you feel the heat from the sun

God's favor is shone upon everyone, and

As the wind blows air across your face

So does mercy surround you because of God's grace

Just as grass grows without seed

So does God supply all of our needs, and

Like without worry the sparrows eat

So upon our table God places meat

Everything that we see and feel

God allows just because of His will,

Never ponder where your blessings come from

Just always thank God for His Begotten Son.

Spiritual Mathematics

God accepted 1 sacrifice for sin

So that you and I could begin again,

It was 2 little fish that fed the thousands, and

3 Hebrews Boys who stood in the fires

4 God so loved the world He gave, and

'Twas 5 loaves of bread, that finally saved,

The multitude who needed to be fed, and

6 is <u>half</u> of the Apostles, that Jesus led

I know this may sound funny to you

But don't worry this poem is almost through,

Remember, God formed the world in only 7 days

This is spiritual mathematics of God's amazing ways.

Sandra Jackson

To My Dad, Elder Nathaniel Lawson

My Dad

My dad is more than a father to me

He's a friend and a kind loving voice,

Each day he prays that I'm O.K.

And that I always make Jesus my choice

He's there when I need to talk to him

And he's always glad I called,

Whether to ask for his advice

Or just for no reason at all

How blessed I am to have someone

Who loves unconditionally,

He helped bring me into the world

And he means just that to me!

My Aunt Ruby

Aunt Ruby is my special Aunt

She's very beautiful but doesn't flaunt,

She's also wise for she fears God, and

Keeps His commandments as she trods

Honor and respect belongs to her

She exemplifies love at every turn,

"Her children rise up and call her blessed"

These are just a few reasons why she's the best!

Sandra Jackson

My Brothers

Let me tell you something about my brothers

I have four of them, and they're like no other,

As I was growing up, they protected me, and

Gave me advice on how other boys should be

First there's Bill, the oldest of them all

He was more like a father, and taught me to stand tall,

Next there's Garfield, the intellectual one

He helped me in 4-H, then to college he had gone

Bob is the third one, a big teddy bear

Sad faces disappeared, whenever he was there,

Horace is the youngest, Mr. GQ

It rubbed off on my son, cause he's like that too

My prayer is that, we never break the ties

That bind our hearts, and strengthen our minds,

I'll always believe that they're a wonder

Lord I thank you for my four brothers!

Sandra Jackson

To My Sister-in-Law, Rossetta

Sister

I'm Oh, so glad you married my brother

He's very happy indeed,

Yet my happiness, isn't only for him

For you're also a great sister to me

Time and time again, while growing

I often wished I had,

A sister I could laugh with and talk to

Though brothers weren't so bad

Now my wish has come true

Sister, you're truly rare,

Cause I could not have picked one better

You're the best sister, anywhere!

Friends

A friend is a blessing directly from God

They're there when things go wrong,

Always hoping and praying for you

There to say, keep holding on

Many people have come and gone

Yet very few stuck around,

Throughout the good and bad times

Till my heart was filled with song

You have proven to be such a friend

Someone who's proven true,

Have always encouraged, "You Better Praise Him!"

Now Sis. Holmes; this praise is for you!

77

Sandra Jackson

Friendship

Whoever Louella McVey may touch

With her caring life,

Becomes a happier person and friend

To this lady who's really nice

I am so very proud to say

She is a friend of mine,

Like the friends of long ago

Completely genuine

In a time where sometimes differences

Causes people to fight,

Our differences somehow draw us close

Whether age or black and white

The benefits of a merry heart

Are discussed within the scriptures,

We've both been very blessed by them

Our friendship keeps us in stitches!

A Special Place

Let me tell you about a place

That is a real life utopia,

People there don't <u>speak</u> of love

They take great pride in showing you

This place posses great qualities

That the whole world should have,

Qualities you can't buy or sell

But should be spread across this land

Unselfishness, caring and sharing

Full of hope, love and faith,

No, there aren't any mansions there

The <u>people</u> make this place

I won't keep you in suspense for long

I hope you take a pilgrimage,

To a place – where friends of mine live

It's called Teresa Village.

Your Friend,

Sandra Jackson

Sandra Jackson

Family

Families evolve around one word

One word, and it is love,

Love is talked and sung about today

Yet, how often is it showed

Scripture says that God is love

Love which is patient and kind,

Long-suffering, enduring all things

Without a puffed up mind

Show me a family without God, and

I'll show you a family in trouble,

When, however, God is their source

Blessings are then doubled

What I guess, I'm trying to say

Is that all things, need a foundation,

If God is allowed to be just that

He'll bless our families and nation.

Contentment

I use to think, every door of opportunity

Gauged just how much, God was blessing me,

But God doesn't measure, success quite the same

For, "Godliness with <u>contentment</u>, is great gain."

So whenever I come across, any closed door

Perhaps God's telling me, less is more,

Sometimes we're measured, by riches and wealth

Yet true riches are family, friends and health

So no matter what anyone, else may think

To be content, is more priceless than mink,

For when this world, shall soon pass away

Having Jesus will be, what counts on that day.

Election 2000

Democrat or Republican

We're all in need of prayer,

Even self proclaimed atheists cry

Oh God! When in despair

Election 2000 taught me that

God's definitely in control,

There has never been a closer race

In history, I am told

Our next U.S. President

Whoever it may be,

Will need full support from the nation

This refers to you and me

So whichever way you might have voted

Let's try hard not to complain,

*For, "…except the Lord, keep the city

The watchman waketh, but in vain."

Sandra Jackson

Fort Walton Beach, Florida

*Psalm 127:1

We Must

It hurts to think that in the minds of children

Are hate, violence and death,

Moanings such as loneliness, distrust

And feelings of worthlessness

How many teachers and children must die

Before we realize our plight,

Not recognizing one child's pain

Results in a war we can't fight

Someone's rights they said had been violated

When we allowed prayer in our schools, but

Now a dark spirit conjures among us

I believe as a nation, we've been fooled

For only God can heal emotional wounds

Which are never in plain sight,

We must again, start praying to Him

For He's the only one, who can make things right.

I Owe

I owe for my life; every breath that I take

I owe for my limbs; each movement they make

I owe for my sight; every dawning I see

I owe for my mind; each trial endured in peace

I owe for my salvation; every sin I overcome

I owe for my victory; each battle Christ has won,

I owe for my long-suffering; every burden I'm able to bare

I owe for my assurance; each problem answered through prayer

I owe for my Church Shepherd; every word God instructs him

to preach

I owe for my fellow servants; each praise I hear them speak,

I owe for my present enemies; every tear they cause me to shed

I owe for my close friends; each day I know they care

I owe my all

I owe my life

I owe because God gave Jesus Christ.

Count Down

Count down till the day Jesus comes

So much to do that hasn't been done,

Here's a count down we can use

Must start now, He's coming soon

-10   Keep yourself free from sin

- 9   Hold on tight until the end

- 8   Keep your hands upon the plow

- 7   Always look up and never down

- 6   Fight the good fight of faith

- 5   Walk with God (don't lose your place)

- 4   Stand up tall no matter the sum

- 3   Keep praying and fasting till morning comes

- 2   Win a soul unto Christ

- 1   Give God your mind, body and life

- 0   Live eternally with Jesus Our Lord

Blast Off   Be part of the Rapture and weep no more!

Just A Note...

Just a note to encourage you

To keep looking up,

There's nothing too hard for God

He's a very present help

For when it seems the darkest

That's when He shines the best,

Baring all our burdens, and

Conquering every test

When it seems that He's not near

Know He hears and sees, and

Surrounded you with love of family

Also friends who care like me

(For we walk by faith, not by sight: 2 Corinthians 5:7)

About the Author

Sandra Jackson is a wife and mother of three teenage boys. She resides in Fort Walton Beach, Florida; where her husband of eighteen years serves in the military. Sandra has been writing since the age of thirteen; and has found love and inspiration in God, her family, and friends. She also has poems published through the Library of Poetry.